South and West from Waterloo

GERRY NICHOLS with photographs by **MARK B. WARBURTON**

Ian Allan
PUBLISHING

First published 2014

ISBN 978 0 7110 3795 3

Published by Ian Allan Publishing Ltd, Hersham, Surrey KT12 4RG.

Printed in China

Visit the Ian Allan Publishing website at **www.ianallanpublishing.com**

Copyright

Photographs
All the photographs in this book were taken by Mark B. Warburton.

FRONT COVER On the afternoon of Wednesday 18 May 1966 'Merchant Navy' 4-6-2 No 35008 *Orient Line* and 'West Country' No 34100 *Appledore* await the right away from Waterloo with trains bound for Bournemouth and Exeter respectively. A Birmingham/Sulzer Type 3 diesel is lurking in the platform between them awaiting the signal to proceed. On the right can be seen the familiar sight of a surburban electric set, at this time with just the lower yellow warning panel.

BACK COVER On the morning of Saturday 19th August 1961, 'Battle of Britain' 4-6-2 34054 *Lord Beaverbrook* is under light steam on the falling gradient approaching Axminster with a down express train. The train is about to pass under the skew bridge carrying the A358 Chard to Axminster road which here follows the alignment of the Roman Fosse Way between Exeter and Leicester. The quarry on the left lies between the A358 and the railway line and supplied material for the works adjacent to the River Axe via a narrow gauge tramway under the line where there was a siding called Coaxdon Siding. At various times this traded as the Dorset Blue Lias Lime and Cement Works and the Exeter Brick and Tile Company. The railway line follows the valley of the River Axe from the summit at Hewish near Crewkerne to just before Seaton Junction when it swings to the west to climb to Honiton.

TITLE PAGE On the same occasion (Wednesday 18 May 1966) as the image on the front cover, 'West Country' 4-6-2 No 34100 *Appledore* awaits the right away from Waterloo Platform 9 with a Salisbury train at the end of the evening rush hour. Considering this is within six weeks of the end of steam on the Southern and its withdrawal on 9 July, No 34100 is clean and still has a nameplate. It was a Salisbury engine from September 1963 and was in good condition as it hauled the 7.46am from Salisbury the following morning giving Mark a 3½ minute early arrival at Waterloo.

Foreword

The Railways

The London & Southampton Railway was one of the first four main lines in southern England; being contemporary with the Great Western line from London to Bristol, the London & Birmingham Railway and the London & Brighton Railway. It was renamed the London & South Western Railway (LSWR) by the 1839 Act of Parliament that also authorised the line from Eastleigh to Gosport, which, according to Dendy Marshall in his *History of the Southern Railway*, was to placate 'the strong objection in Portsmouth to that town being served by a company in whose name the rival port of Southampton was so prominent'. The extent of its ambitions may be appreciated by its purchase in 1847 of the Bodmin & Wadebridge Railway which had opened in 1834, but was not joined to the rest of the South Western system until 1895 when the North Cornwall line was opened between Delabole and Wadebridge. There are both comprehensive and popular histories of the London & South Western Railway that describe the frequent battles with the broad gauge railways (Great Western, Bristol & Exeter and Cornwall Railways) in the development of the network to the south at Dorchester and to the west at Plymouth, Padstow, Bude and Ilfracombe.

By 1908 the first 50 miles from Waterloo to beyond Basingstoke had been quadrupled with flying junctions to segregate through, local and branching services. The junction between the Southampton and Salisbury lines was relocated to Worting Junction signalbox, about ³/₄ mile east of the site of the original junction, and the superseding flyover at Battledown that is illustrated in the album. In this distance from Waterloo, the line climbed more or less steadily to an elevation of 375 feet above sea level. However, from here the Southampton line, once over the summit short of Micheldever, falls continuously for 28 miles to Southampton joining the valley of the River Itchen from Winchester. From Southampton the line undulates as it crosses the river valleys around the north of the New Forest to the Hampshire Avon at Christchurch; whence a steep climb takes it to Bournemouth Central, and an even steeper fall through Parkstone to return it to near sea level at Poole. Beyond Poole the valley of the Dorset Frome is joined at Wareham and the line rises steadily to Dorchester before the final descent to Weymouth, 143 miles from Waterloo.

The line to the west, from Worting Junction, has a very different character as the route, as far as Exeter, crosses a series of river valleys running north to south. This saw-tooth profile meant steam locomotives could mortgage the boiler on the uphill sections and recover as gravity assisted on the downhill sections. With the Bulleid Pacifics, the line limit of 80mph was frequently exceeded even with trains of 400 tons. All trains stopped at Salisbury, 83 miles from Waterloo, to change crews and fill the tender with water. This caused significant engineering problems as all trains started from the same place and the predilection of Bulleid Pacifics to slip on starting caused significant wear, with the rails needing frequent replacement. Beyond Exeter (171 miles from Waterloo), the line to Barnstaple utilised the Yeo and Taw valleys while the Plymouth line skirted the northern edge of Dartmoor before using the Tavy and Tamar valleys. The North Cornwall line from Halwill Junction to Wadebridge and Padstow (259 miles from Waterloo) was, like the Great Western Fishguard route, justifiable only as part of a through route. Like many small branches under the Beeching analysis, it was uneconomic on the local traffic it could generate, especially as car use became more widespread and restrictions on commercial vans and lorries were removed. Finally, in time and significance, came the North Devon & Cornwall Junction Railway between Halwill Junction and Torrington authorised in 1914 but not opened until 1925 and destined to have a life of only 40 years.

Prior to 1964 the pattern of railway services on these lines was little changed from the practices of the old Western Division of the Southern Railway. Significant improvements had been made by the Southern Railway in rebuilding stations such as Yeovil and Seaton Junctions to separate through lines from platform lines. The main line expresses were steam-operated and called at principal stations about every 75 miles. This was necessary as there were no water troughs but also convenient as semi-fast and local services could provide connections to and from intermediate stations. Motive power from the pre-grouping era disappeared in the early 1960s, when completion of the Kent electrification meant an influx of more modern types of steam locomotive, and the headlong rush of the Western Region into diesel-hydraulics and diesel multiple-units released both rolling stock and locomotives. The dieselisation of the Lymington Pier branch on 3 April 1967 (although the Hampshire units were replaced by electric units on 2 June 1967) and completion of Bournemouth electrification on 10 July 1967 saw the end of steam on the Southern Region.

The Photographer

Mark B. Warburton was born and educated in Bristol, living for the first 50 years of his life in Brislington almost equidistant between St Anne's Park station on the Great Western main line and Brislington station on the North Somerset line to Radstock and Frome. After a period of National Service, he worked as a Dues Clerk for the Port of Bristol Authority collecting the payments for the use of the Docks from the ships' master. This had the great advantage of him being out of the office for much of the working day, giving ample opportunities for photographing excursion trains to Clifton Down for Bristol Zoo! Accepting the offer of early retirement in 1981, he subsequently married Margaret and they set up home in Longwell Green. He greatly enjoyed his step family and enjoyed an active retirement. After a serious operation shortly after his 80th birthday in August 2011, he was bed-bound and died on 27 November 2011.

Mark's railway interests were evident from an early age and he found kindred spirits in Bristol Railway Circle, later also joining the Railway Correspondence & Travel Society and the Stephenson Locomotive Society. He rapidly became interested in the more obscure branch lines of South Wales and the South West of England, travelling by train and bicycle to try to emulate T. R. Perkins in travelling on all the lines open to passengers. He also became interested in train timing and the effective demise of express steam on the Great Western meant travel on the Southern Region Western Division particularly using Rail Rover tickets to spend a week behind Bulleid Pacifics on the Bournemouth and Exeter trains. He published several articles on these experiences and his logs have been bequeathed to the Railway Performance Society. Except for single visits to Switzerland and Northern Ireland and regular visits to the Isle of Man, he never travelled outside British mainland.

We are fortunate that Mark not only recorded the railway scene photographically and ensured that his slides had the date and place on them but also maintained a railway diary or trip book so that the context of most of the pictures can be explained. These books are all marked 'Confidential Not to be loaned' and one felt extremely privileged to be allowed to see them under supervision during Mark's lifetime. As an author, I am grateful to Margaret for being allowed access to these documents, which enable the captions to be both accurate and informative.

The Photographs

Mark had been an active railway photographer as soon as he could afford it, taking many black and white photographs, particularly of GWR branch lines in the 1950s. Within Bristol Railway Circle at that time, there were good photographers such as Godfrey Soole, S. Miles Davey and Maurice Deane and the annual photographic competition was a good training and testing ground. Mark showed considerable talent in picture composition although there was one occasion when the judge of the photographic competition took a dislike to some cows in the foreground with the remark 'Perutz green grass and Agfa brown cows!!' – see what you think (see page 62).

As will be evident from the selection, most of his photographs were taken incidentally to his interest in railway travel being taken in or around stations where he was making a train connection, although on occasions he would participate in a lineside observation day with others – hence the Battledown series of pictures on 25 July 1964 for instance. On other occasions he would spend an hour at a station having a break from a car journey in those pre-motorway days. However he never had a great interest in London's railways nor did he attempt to make a photographic record of them. Hence there are few images available east of Basingstoke. Rail access from Bristol was easiest to Exeter or Salisbury, or using excursions over the Somerset & Dorset Joint Railway line to Bournemouth. These allowed ample time to explore the Weymouth line and the Swanage and Lymington branches.

Some of his earliest colour pictures are taken on the line through Brislington, which lost its passenger service in November 1959 – this seems to have been the spur to record what would soon be disappearing. Also at that time, colour film was improving from the 4ASA speed rating (exposure a fortnight at f8!!) to more useable speeds, which enabled photography of moving trains in less than ideal lighting. Mark used 35mm Agfa CT18 for many years, which has meant that his transparencies have had to be colour corrected despite having been kept at room temperature in lightproof boxes. Considering many of the transparencies are now over 50 years old, they have survived well.

Unlike his black and white pictures, which appeared in *Trains Annual* and the *Railway Magazine*, Mark's colour images were not published in his lifetime. We surmise that he was not willing to allow the slides to be copied or to send the original transparency to a publisher because of the possibility of them being lost or damaged. Very occasionally a selection would appear at Bristol Railway Circle slide shows but few of us realised what a treasure trove of images it comprised. Mark's widow Margaret has been very generous in allowing me to scan the slides and make them available for publication, always with the proviso that the standards must be good enough to meet Mark's very high standards.

Acknowledgements

The generosity and co-operation of Margaret Warburton in making available the slides is gratefully acknowledged. I am also pleased to acknowledge the encouragement of Kevin Robertson and the staff at Ian Allan Publishing at Hersham in the production of this album.

On various occasions members of Bristol Railway Circle and the Bristol Group of the Historical Model Railway Society have seen some of these images and I have been considerably educated by the ensuing discussion – it never ceases to amaze me how a fresh pair of eyes can see something completely new in a familiar picture.

London to Weymouth

Returning from a week's holiday in Sussex on Saturday 25 August 1962, Mark broke the car journey with an hour on Basingstoke station. Here looking west from the station platform to Basingstoke shed, 'Modified Hall' 4-6-0 No 6927 *Lilford Hall* (allocated to Old Oak Common) has the shunting signal to come off the shed, the signalman having been rung from the adjacent telephone. An 'S15' 4-6-0 simmers in the distance with the stock for an up local, while visible on shed are a Type 3 (later Class 33) diesel and a Drummond 0-6-0. Basingstoke shed was closed in 1967 and demolished in 1969.

'West Country' 4-6-2 No 34092 *City of Wells* sweeps through Basingstoke on 25 August 1962 with an up West of England express raising the dust and dirt. The fireman is taking a breather with 15 miles of falling gradients to come have done most of the hard work in the first 10 miles climbing from Salisbury to Grateley. The reporting number 260 is not pasted on a headcode disc but on a separate plate hung from the upper lamp bracket and secured to the side lamp brackets with string. Happily No 34092 is still with us having been withdrawn in November 1964. After a period operating on the Keighley & Worth Valley, it is hoped to restore it to steam shortly following overhaul.

'Schools' 4-4-0 No 30925 *Cheltenham* pulls into Basingstoke on Saturday 25 August 1962 to take water whilst working an up special boat train, also known as a Ocean Liner Express, from Southampton Docks via Northam to Waterloo. Mark recorded the load as 13 coaches, including two Pullmans visible as the second and third vehicles. This would allow the First Class passengers to walk out of the gates onto the taxi road at Waterloo! No 30925 was, of course, for many years the particular mascot of the Railway Correspondence & Travel Society, a line drawing featuring at the head of the *Railway Observer*. This may have influenced its choice for preservation as part of the National Collection on withdrawal at the end of 1962. It was an Eastern Division locomotive based at Dover or Bricklayers Arms until Kent electrification sent it to the Western Division. It appeared in steam in the Rainhill Cavalcade in 1980 and, after restoration at Knight Rail, Eastleigh, is now on loan from the National Railway Museum to the Mid Hants Railway.

We have now come to Worting Junction, west of Basingstoke on a rather overcast Saturday 24 August 1963 when Mark stopped off for a two-hour break en-route from Bristol to Southsea. Between midday and 2pm, 18 down and 21 up trains passed and approximately half changed tracks at the junction.

Looking east, 'Battle of Britain' 4-6-2 No 34073 *249 Squadron* is working the 12.35pm Waterloo to Weymouth with 11 coaches and is five minutes behind schedule. Speed will have come down to 60mph for the crossover visible in the next picture, which will take it onto the Southampton line. The buildings in the background show clear railway origins and are a reminder of the labour needed to maintain the permanent way.

Looking west a few minutes earlier, GWR 4-6-0 No 6851 *Hurst Grange* is rolling down from the Battledown flyover visible in the background with the nine coaches of the 11.36am Bournemouth West to Manchester Victoria running seven minutes early. A year earlier this train would have worked north over the Somerset & Dorset Joint Railway. The train is signalled onto the up slow line past Worting Junction signalbox with the up 9.10am Torrington to Waterloo train signalled on the fast lines.

Saturday 25 July 1964 was a lineside watch, by members of Bristol Railway Circle, adjacent to Battledown flyover at Worting Junction. Between 10am and 4pm they saw 92 trains: 29 of the 45 down trains and 35 of the 47 up trains were steam-hauled.

LEFT 'Battle of Britain' 4-6-2 No 34079 *141 Squadron* swings under the Battledown flyover with the four coaches of the 12.06 Salisbury to Waterloo running three minutes late but with plenty of leeway to make up time given a reasonable road. The grass in the foreground shows evidence of both work by the permanent way staff in keeping it down and the spark throwing capability of Bulleid Pacifics. No 34079 had initially been allocated to Ramsgate but had moved west to Exmouth Junction in 1958 before being re-allocated to Eastleigh in September 1964 and being withdrawn in July 1966.

LEFT 'Battle of Britain' 4-6-2 No 34064 *Fighter Command* climbs up to cross the West of England line with the nine coaches of the 9.32am Bournemouth Central to Waterloo with the Worting Junction distant at caution. This will not help the timekeeping, it being six minutes late at this stage. The spark throwing property of the Bulleid Pacifics was one reason why this engine was rebuilt with the Giesl ejector spark arrester at a General Overhaul in 1962. While this was successful both in reduced fire raising and increased power output, it came too late for the cost to be justifiable for further installations.

LEFT 'West Country' 4-6-2 No 34038 *Lynton* is in charge of the 12.14 Waterloo to Bournemouth West comprising nine coaches with six minutes to make up on the schedule at this point. The soft exhaust of the Bulleid Pacific under light steam means that the abutment of the bridge behind is clearly visible above the top electric lamp on the cowl.

LEFT The broadside view of 'Battle of Britain' 4-6-2 No 34057 *Biggin Hill* gives a splendid impression of speed and power. The train is the 10.35 Waterloo to Padstow and Bude and it has already lost 12 minutes on schedule with its load of 10 coaches. The fireman is taking a breather with the hard work on the long ascent nearly over and the safety valves nicely lifting. Judging by the trimming of the coal he has already shovelled at least one ton of the five-ton capacity.

LEFT With the safety valves lifting indicating spare steam despite the deplorable external condition of the engine, Standard Class 5 4-6-0 No 73074 hauls the 9.05am Wolverhampton to Portsmouth train on the Southampton line at Battledown. Running more than 15 minutes late, there may be an opportunity to haul back some of those minutes on the descent to Eastleigh where it will swing onto the Fareham line. The rake of 11 coaches has clearly been assembled from the back of the coach sidings as it would appear no two coaches have the same profile.

LEFT The down 'Bournemouth Belle' (12.30 Waterloo to Bournemouth West) with a uniform rake of 12 Pullman cars is in charge of 'Merchant Navy' 4-6-2 No 35022 *Holland America Line* and has a mere two minutes to make up on schedule. The driver is keeping an eye on the lineside watchers and again the exhaust is so light that it does not obscure the bridge abutments behind the chimney. In the foreground are two of the products of the Exmouth Junction concrete works - the standard permanent way hut on the right and the smaller lockup hut on the left.

In the last full summer of steam operation, 'West Country' 4-6-2 No 34037 *Clovelly* is working quite hard as it passes Micheldever with the 8.30am from Waterloo on 20 August 1966. The blue and grey livery has started to appear in the form of the leading brake 3rd although the rest of the train visible is green. The third rail for electrification is in place on both up and down lines and the permanent way wagon in the foreground looks to contain spare sleepers and crossing timbers.

ABOVE Looking north from the down platform of Winchester City station on 18 August 1962, 'Merchant Navy' 4-6-2 No 35011 *General Steam Navigation*, the 11am Bournemouth to Waterloo has the road but awaits the right away with the safety valves lifting – plenty of steam for the pull up the 1 in 245 gradient to Micheldever with its 10 coaches. Meanwhile 'Schools' 4-4-0 No 30903 *Charterhouse* approaches with the 11.22am Waterloo to Weymouth hoping to make up some time despite its load of 11 coaches. Both services were running 18 minutes late on schedule on this day. On the right can be seen one of the hexagonal lampshades giving a very 1930s flavour to a 1960s scene.

FACING PAGE TOP A two-hour lunch break en route by car to Bristol from Eastbourne on Saturday 24 August 1962 gave a further opportunity to watch trains at Winchester City. Here 'West Country' 4-6-2 No 34100 *Appledore* approaches with the 10.42am Poole to Sheffield Midland train which was booked to stop at Winchester. It is good to see from the cover picture at

Waterloo taken eight months later that underneath the grime was a sound engine that worked to the very end of steam on the Southern. Once again the London Midland Region has assembled a variety of stock for the 10 coaches from the back of the carriage sidings although it is more uniform than some!

FACING PAGE BOTTOM BR Standard Class 5 4-6-0 No 73082 (at one time named *Camelot*) pulls out of the down loop sidings at Winchester City on Saturday 24 August 1965 with an engineer's train having the road after the 10.45 Waterloo to Swanage has passed. In the up platform the two-car diesel unit (out of sight to the left) forming the train to Alton has the road but has not finished its station work. The smokebox of the engine looks as though char has been allowed to accumulate and catch fire although the front fall plate shows evidence of emptying of the smokebox. In the siding on the right is an intriguing vehicle, possibly some sort of mobile generator? Anyway it does not merit any attention from the young train spotters on the right.

ABOVE A delightful study of the station pilot at Winchester City on Monday 26 August 1963 slumbering behind the up platform with the shunter's pole parked across the rear lamp irons. 'B4' 0-4-0T No 30096 was 70 years old at the time and was to have further useful life, being purchased by Corralls to shunt Dibles Wharf, Northam, Southampton, on withdrawal by British Railways two months later. From there it was purchased by the Bulleid Preservation Society in 1972 and moved to the Bluebell Railway. Built at Nine Elms in the Adams era it was named *Normandy*, and the original partly open cabsheets were closed in during World War 2 to reduce glare from the firebox. The original rear cab-sheet profile can be seen in this rear view and has been restored in preservation.

FACING PAGE TOP From what is now a car park for Southampton International Airport, 'Merchant Navy' 4-6-2 No 35014 *Nederland Line* is seen passing Eastleigh Works with the 10.30am Waterloo to Bournemouth service on 18 April 1964. This was the occasion of the Locomotive Club of Great Britain

'Hampshire Venturer' railtour which started from Portsmouth and included a visit to the Works en route to Salisbury, Fordingbridge and Southampton. The housing on the left in Southampton Road is part of the railway town established between 1891 and 1910 as the carriage and wagon and then locomotive works were built adjacent to what had been previously known as Bishopstoke Junction.

FACING PAGE BOTTOM BR Standard Class 4 4-6-0 No 75077 fitted with a double-chimney drifts through Swaythling station with a down boat train on Saturday 20 August 1966. Swaythling station was opened in 1883 as Swathling, the extra 'y' being added in 1895 at the request of the squire Sir Samuel Montagu. On the right edge of the picture can be seen the covered way to the station building which was set back so that an extra track could be installed on the down side, but never was. The houses on the left were demolished for the construction of Thomas Lewis Way, which was opened in 1988 as a bypass for the Portswood Road into Southampton from the M27.

Mark paid a visit to a number of locations on the Bournemouth line on 20 August 1966 at the end of what was expected, and proved to be, the final summer of steam.

LEFT 'West Country' 4-6-2 No 34102 *Lapford* pauses for water in Southampton Central station with a Waterloo train. No 34102 was to be one of the few unrebuilt engines to last to the end of steam in July 1967. Two platforms to the west of the original 1895 Southampton station were added in the mid-1930s as is evidenced by the design of the footbridge. The station clock tower was demolished in 1967 to be replaced by a totally anonymous office block.

RIGHT BR Class 9F 2-10-0 No 92002 takes water at Southampton Central, heading the Poole to Newcastle train, bearing the very unofficial name of 'King Rat'! The formation of 11 coaches includes a Restaurant Car and two coaches in the blue and grey livery. The engine was shedded at Banbury and would presumably have worked the down train satisfactorily hence being rostered for the return to its home shed.

RIGHT 'West Country' 4-6-2 No 34017 *Ilfracombe* pulls into Southampton Central with the 10.30am from Waterloo. The conductor rails are in place although not in use. Ivatt 2-6-2T No 41319 on station pilot duty simmers in down headshunt while a number of Southampton Corporation Transport buses in their smart crimson and cream livery pass along the Western Esplanade. The Esplanade was the waterfront at the time of the opening of the station in 1895, all the land to the present waterfront was reclaimed as part of the Docks. In the left at the background can be seen the monumental clock tower of the Civic Centre.

ABOVE On a later visit 'West Country' 4-6-2 No 34008 (formerly *Padstow*, but with nameplate and crest of Cornish bezants removed) awaits the road at the down end of Southampton Central with the 10.30am Waterloo to Bournemouth on Wednesday 29 March 1967. The following week this particular service was scheduled to be an electric service, so Mark travelled down from Waterloo behind No 34008 which had worked its 10-coach train well until a series of signal checks between Eastleigh and Southampton (caused Mark suspected by the lack of platform availability at Southampton following the closure of Southampton Terminus station and the diversion of Alton and Reading trains to Central).

FACING PAGE TOP BR Standard Class 4 2-6-0 No 76011 pulls out of Southampton Central station past the 1934-built signalbox with a down parcels train on 29 March 1967.

FACING PAGE BOTTOM In the late afternoon of a wet August Bank Holiday Monday, 6 August 1962, GWR 4-6-0 No 5990 *Dorford Hall* steams through Brockenhurst with the Newcastle to Bournemouth train. The signalbox and level crossing visible in the background on the Lymington Road are adjacent to the station buildings on the down side, from which the green corrugated iron covered way leads to the station footbridge. Brockenhurst is the junction station for the Lymington branch although the actual junction is just under a mile further west.

ABOVE BR Standard Class 4 2-6-4T No 80146 is on the Lymington Pier to Brockenhurst service on 29 March 1967 and takes water at Brockenhurst on arrival, before running round its two coaches for a return working. A headboard was carried in this last week of operation to the effect that this was the last steam worked branch line on British Railways. The following week it was operated by two-car Hampshire diesel multiple-units and they were turn superseded by electric units on 2 June 1967.

FACING PAGE TOP 'West Country' 4-6-2 No 34004 *Yeovil* approaches Lymington Junction signalbox having just passed through Brockenhurst station with the eight coaches of a Waterloo to Bournemouth train on 20 August 1966. The conductor rail is in place but not yet energised. In the background can be seen wild ponies grazing alongside the Sway road and the open countryside is typical of the scenery through this area of the New Forest.

FACING PAGE BOTTOM BR Standard Class 4 2-6-4T No 80019 pulls out of Lymington Town station with a Lymington Pier to Brockenhurst train on 20 July 1966. The sidings have been lifted in the yard but the line to the goods shed is in place, although the goods service had been withdrawn in August 1965. The buildings here date from 1860, although the line was extended to the Pier station in 1884.

FACING PAGE TOP The driver of BR Standard Class 4 2-6-4T No 80151 is pulling forward very carefully to run round its Manchester RTS special train of five coaches at Lymington Pier on 25 March 1967. The normal service train used the bay platform on this occasion, possibly the last time it was used. The locomotive is carrying the 'Hants & Dorset Branch Flyer' headboard, the top of which can be seen above the front of the smokebox and this accounts for the engine working chimney first down the branch, the reverse of the normal direction. The margin for error with a locomotive this long was small as the locomotive buffers had nearly to touch the stop to clear the point blades. This was an exposed location in bad weather and there were few regrets from operating staff with the end of steam.

FACING PAGE BOTTOM BR Standard Class 4 2-6-4T No 80146 was seen previously taking water at Brockenhurst and here it is ready to depart from Lymington Pier on 29 March 1967. The arms of the rail-built signal look to be of LSWR origin and Lymington Pier signalbox can just be seen in the distance.

ABOVE Meanwhile back on the main line, 'West Country' 4-6-2 No 34006 *Bude* is seen starting its Waterloo-bound train from Sway station on Saturday 20 August 1966. Despite the rising gradient and a train of 10 coaches, the steam sanders are not in use and there is no sign of slipping. This engine was one of three fitted with extra long smoke deflectors in 1948 but the other two lost them on being rebuilt. *Bude* was a star performer on the Great Central line in the 1948 Interchange trials recording over 2,000 drawbar horsepower albeit with heavy coal consumption.

FACING PAGE TOP 'Merchant Navy' 4-6-2 No 35013 *Blue Funnel Line* brings the down 'Bournemouth Belle' past New Milton on the 20 August 1966. This engine, in the last week of steam operation, allegedly reached 106mph, but was withdrawn and scrapped. The blue and grey full brake rather spoils the appearance of the train against the Pullman car livery of the remaining vehicles. Here the conductor rail is not yet in place on the down line although the rail has been unloaded in the four foot ready to be mounted on the insulators. The tall structure on the right is a water tower erected in 1900 to resemble (unsuccessfully) a castle keep.

FACING PAGE BOTTOM 'Merchant Navy' 4-6-2 No 35005 *Canadian Pacific* sweeps past Christchurch station on time with the down 'Bournemouth Belle' on 16 March 1964. While not ideal conditions for crisp colour pictures, this picture has been included to illustrate the effect at speed of the bluff smokebox front in creating an eddy in front of the chimney

and the ability of the smoke deflectors to lift the steam keeping good forward visibility for the driver. In fact on this date, the engine failed at Bournemouth with a hot big end bearing and 'West Country' 4-6-2 No 34045 *Ottery St Mary* worked the return train, arriving at Waterloo only two minutes late despite a 20mph permanent way slowing at Winchester. Having been rescued from Barry scrapyard, No 35005 is now in store at Eastleigh under cover awaiting overhaul being owned by the Mid Hants Railway.

ABOVE 'West Country' 4-6-2 No 34022 *Exmoor* pulls into the up platform at Bournemouth Central in the late afternoon of Bank Holiday Monday, 5 August 1963, with a return North of England train. This train would have travelled by the Somerset & Dorset Joint Railway the previous year but now will make its way north via Basingstoke, Reading and Oxford. Mark and others had travelled from Bath by an excursion over the Somerset & Dorset to Bournemouth.

ABOVE Turning round having taken the previous picture from the down platform at Bournemouth Central, here is a general view of Bournemouth shed with LSWR 'M7' 0-4-4T No 30048, BR Standard Class 4 2-6-4T No 80081 and unidentified 'S15' 4-6-0, BR Standard 4-6-0 and a rebuilt Bulleid Pacific also visible. The crossing at the right of the picture was quite steeply graded, being a favourite place for a Bulleid Pacific to demonstrate its light footedness even when running as a light engine. The considerable length of the down platform can be appreciated from the right hand edge of the previous picture and the left hand side of this view being nearly a quarter of a mile long and able to take two full length trains.

FACING PAGE TOP LMS Class 5 4-6-0 No 45493 pulls into Poole station with the 11 coaches of the 10.54 Poole-Newcastle service on Saturday 27 August 1966, as Type 3 diesel No D6515 awaits the right away on a down working. At this time, the Newcastle train was the only steam working between Banbury and Basingstoke and the only steam passenger service on

Western Region metals. Mark travelled as far as Oxford on this train, changing there into the return Newcastle train despite a 21-minute late arrival. In the distance on the right can be seen the floodlighting towers of the Wimborne Road Stadium, home of the Poole Pirates speedway team and until 1994 the home ground of Poole Town FC.

FACING PAGE BOTTOM 'Battle of Britain' 4-6-2 No 34064 *Fighter Command* awaits the right away at Wareham with a Weymouth train on Bank Holiday Monday 5 August 1963. The Giesl ejector is more evident in this view of the locomotive than the previous picture at Battledown. Having left the Bath to Bournemouth excursion at Poole to join this train, Mark then joined the Swanage branch train visible in the bay on the right. The two 'M7s' in service on this day were Nos 30108 and 30667 working as usual with the engine at the Wareham end of the two-coach sets. This carriage set, No 612, was one of the adaptations of surplus rolling stock after the Kent electrification, which replaced older coaches on the Western Division.

ABOVE During a holiday in Swanage in July 1966, Mark was able to cover more locations on the Swanage branch starting with the junction with the main line at Worgret Junction on Thursday 21st. Here rebuilt 'West Country' 4-6-2 No 34017 *Ilfracombe,* in filthy condition, passes the distinctive signalbox with an up Weymouth to Waterloo train. The height of the up home signal for visibility over the cutting on the curve will be noted as will the 10mph speed restriction and tablet catching horn for the single line from Swanage in the foreground. The small hut at the bottom of the stairs is presumably the toilet for the signalman!

LEFT Ivatt 2-6-2T No 41230 passes the remains of the Pike Brothers' Norden clay works with a Swanage to Wareham train late in the afternoon of Thursday 21 July 1966. The embankment formation of the bridge carrying the 2ft 8½in gauge line from the Norden clay mines over the Swanage branch can be identified but the girders of the bridge have already been removed. On the left can be seen some of the narrow gauge wagons on the line that led to the trans-shipment shed and standard gauge siding located behind the photographer. The distinctive ruins of Corfe Castle dominate the gap in the Purbeck Hills exploited by road and rail to Swanage.

ABOVE Here is the classic view of 'M7' 0-4-4T No 30667 propelling its coaches towards the Studland road viaduct on the approach to Corfe Castle from Wareham as seen from the castle. The solitary road vehicle in sight on a Bank Holiday Monday (5 August 1963) almost beggars belief. In the distance can be seen Poole Harbour and the red brick of Poole Power Station on Holes Bay, with the dark green of the western end of Brownsea Island also visible to the right.

ABOVE On Saturday 23 July, Ivatt 2-6-2T No 41230 stops in Corfe Castle station and a party of children disembark. It has been turned since being photographed two days earlier now chimney first towards Swanage. It will be noted that push pull operation had been dispensed with involving the locomotive running round the train at both Swanage and Wareham. Behind the running in board on the left can be glimpsed one of the two Pullman Camping Coaches on the siding behind the station house. Earlier photographs show that for the 1961 season only one Pullman Coach was there, but that had become two by the 1963 season.

FACING PAGE TOP BR Standard Class 4 2-6-4T No 80134 approaches the bridge under the main Corfe Castle to Swanage road with the down empty coach stock for a through Swanage to Waterloo train on Saturday 23 July 1966. The eight coaches were the maximum that could be accommodated in Swanage station

and the train locomotive, 'Battle of Britain' 4-6-2 No 34071 *601 Squadron*, worked down light engine tender-first from Bournemouth shed as it was too long to be turned on the Swanage turntable. This view of Corfe Castle from the south east emphasises the strategic position of the castle mound and how magnificent it must have been before being 'modified' by Oliver Cromwell!

FACING PAGE BOTTOM BR Standard Class 4 2-6-4T No 80085 is signalled into the main platform at Swanage with a train from Wareham on Friday 22 July 1966. The engine shed at Swanage was unusual in that access was only possible over the turntable. The entrance was arched until 1958 when an 'M7' 0-4-4T overshot the turntable and collided with the building, demolishing part of the end wall. The building was repaired with a lintel beam and wooden panelling in the form showed here. This is of course now an active railway again under the auspices of the Swanage Railway.

RIGHT The fireman of rebuilt 'Battle of Britain' 4-6-2 No 34071 *601 Squadron* picks up the single line token from the signalman as it leaves Swanage with one of the two Waterloo trains on Saturday 23 July 1966. Track has been lifted to the goods shed as goods services had been withdrawn the previous year, however the sidings to the right have been retained for carriage stock or in this case for No 80085 to await a path back to Wareham. The other Waterloo train on this Saturday was worked by Type 3 diesel D6517.

RIGHT Finally a general view of Swanage station taken in 1959, clearly in the holiday season to judge by the wet platforms! 'M7' 0-4-4T No 30105 with an augmented push pull set has just arrived as it still has the tail lamp in position on the front buffer beam. Two motor coaches can be seen in the goods yard beyond the carriages in the bay platform, presumably excursion or tour bookings.

ABOVE Meanwhile back on the main line we have reached Wool station and here look west towards Dorchester from the station footbridge. BR Standard Class 4 2-6-0 No 76014 has the road and awaits the right away to restart a Bournemouth to Weymouth train on Friday 22 July 1966. The road crossing the railway is the main A352 from Wareham to Dorchester and, although the gates have been replaced with lifting barriers, the signalbox remains and if you look on Google Maps satellite view you can see cars waiting for the barriers to be lifted! Another contrast in this picture is the more relaxed attitude to road works taking place on the main road before the Health and Safety at Work etc Act 1974 – not a cone or a temporary traffic light to be seen, just two simple notices.

RIGHT 'West Country' 4-6-2 No 34012 *Launceston* has arrived from Weymouth and reversed back into the up platform at Dorchester South with a Waterloo-bound train on Saturday 26 March 1966. The reason for the visit to the area was to see 'A4' No 60024 *Kingfisher* running Waterloo to Weymouth, to Yeovil, to Waterloo on the A4 Preservation Special but the opportunity was taken to photograph en route. Why the Southern persisted with the awkward reversal for so long is not clear, as the opportunity was taken, in 1970, to build an up platform on the curve opposite the down platform from which this photograph was taken.

'Merchant Navy' 4-6-2 No 35013 *Blue Funnel* awaits the road on the 1.25pm Weymouth to Waterloo service on 16 October 1965. The safety valves are lifting so there should be a good head of steam for the climb to Bincombe Tunnel. Mark travelled on this train to Waterloo and noted that the engine was not in the best of mechanical condition. Clearly this was sorted out on the light casual overhaul at the beginning of 1966 as it became a star performer in the last week of steam on the Southern as noted previously. The ornamental scroll work on the gas lamp is notable as it is the plain, rather than barley twist casting of the lamp standard.

Train engine 'Merchant Navy' 4-6-2 No 35019 *French Line CGT* on the 5.35pm Weymouth to Waterloo has a pilot in the form of BR Standard Class 4 2-6-0 No 76056 on Easter Monday 23 April 1962. The tender of the 'Merchant Navy' has been well-filled and, of course, there would be a considerable weight of coal already in the firebox. The pilot only ran as far as Dorchester where, as previous mentioned, the train set back into the up platform so the pilot could be detached. Where trains were banked through Upwey, the banker would be uncoupled and would drop off at Bincombe signalbox before Dorchester to cross over and return to Weymouth. Lighting on this platform had been converted to electricity in 1962 whereas the other platforms seen in the previous picture were still gaslit three years later!

GWR 0-6-0PT No 7782 negotiates the Weymouth Tramway with the 10 coaches, plus van, of the 4pm Channel Island boat train to Waterloo and has encountered a clearance problem. The railway staff are trying to bump a car out of the way - perhaps as it is Bank Holiday Monday 1962, a driver from out of town has parked who is not aware the railway lines are in use. The fashions and cars of 50 years ago are interesting and it is clear that the cyclists are aware of the dangers of crossing the lines at too oblique an angle.

Earlier on Easter Bank Holiday Monday 1962, the same train seen above awaits the right away from Weymouth Quay station. Outside-cylinder 0-6-0PT No 1369, one the locomotives fitted with a bell for working the Tramway, is alongside No 7782 on the Waterloo train, and the newly commissioned SS *Sarnia* is moored discharging its passengers and cargo. Beyond the SS *Sarnia* is the ex-GWR vessel SS *Patrick*. However much of the fascination of this picture is the holiday makers of the period sitting in the foreground and standing on the platform and the variety of stores and equipment behind the railings. Finally for 3 shillings (15p) one could view the ships and submarines of HM Navy from a trip around the harbour with a fully licensed boatman!

Andover to the West

Two photographs taken at Andover Junction on the morning of Saturday 25 July 1964 en route from Bristol to begin the line-side watch at Battledown at 10am.

Rebuilt West Country 4-6-2 No 34003 *Plymouth* rolls under the Millway Road bridge and is signalled into the platform road past Andover Junction B signalbox with an up parcels train. BR Standard Class 5 4-6-0 No 73117 pulls away from Andover Junction station with a down passenger train comprising a three-coach set and two vans past the photographer's red VW Beetle.

'Merchant Navy' 4-6-2 No 35009 *Shaw Savill* restarts the up 'Atlantic Coast Express' (12.30pm from Exeter Central to Waterloo) from Salisbury on Saturday 8 June 1963. To the eight coaches of the Ilfracombe and Torrington portion a further two coaches and a restaurant car had been added at Exeter Central making, with a packed train, a gross load of at least 400 tons. Time had been kept to Salisbury on this day despite signals due to catching up the Padstow and Bude portion, which had left Exeter 10 minutes earlier with only eight coaches. With such a load, the driver has the steam sanders on as the train pulls away.

ABOVE 'Battle of Britain' 4-6-2 No 34057 *Biggin Hill* restarts the Cardiff to Brighton train from Salisbury on Saturday 8 June 1963 without the need to use the steam sanders. The lighter colour of the track on the up main, due to the sand, can be seen clearly and the enginemen ensure that the sanders are off at the end of the checkrail section and before the facing set of points.

FACING PAGE Two magnificent views of 'Battle of Britain' 4-6-2 No 34051 *Winston Churchill* in the west down bay platform of Salisbury station on Thursday 24 October 1963. The engine left Eastleigh Works after its last Light Intermediate overhaul on 12 October 1963, and according to the Engine Record Card having received new-type pistons and crossheads and clearly a repaint. No 34051 was one of Salisbury shed's favourite locomotives and, of course, achieved fame and future preservation in the National Railway Museum collection after being used to haul Sir Winston Churchill's funeral train on 30 January 1965.

ABOVE By way of contrast here is the condition that 'Battle of Britain' 4-6-2 No 34051 *Winston Churchill* was in immediately prior to its overhaul. The location is the summit of the 1 in 100 climb from Templecombe at Stowell with a nine-coach down train on Saturday 3 August 1963 - another three weeks to go before arriving at Eastleigh Works. The Templecombe up distant colour light signal can be seen over the rear coach.

FACING PAGE TOP A magnificent study of 'Battle of Britain' 4-6-2 No 34066 *Spitfire* taking water in the up platform at Yeovil Junction station on Saturday 13 July 1963. The tail lamp would seem to indicate that it will probably run light engine to Yeovil Town shed for servicing. There has been an issue of black gloss paint judging by the barley twist gas

lamps and the running in board supports. In the background adjacent to the east signalbox an 'S15' 4-6-0 approaches tender first with parcels vans from Yeovil Town and Yeovil South Junction.

FACING PAGE BOTTOM 'West Country' 4-6-2 No 34092 *City of Wells* is seen in the up platform at Yeovil Junction on Saturday 28 July 1962. As there was no direct access to this line from the down main, it is believed that this semi-fast down passenger train has terminated in the down platform and drawn forward to the west box and then reversed its coaches into the up platform. The engine has uncoupled and will run round to take the coaches to Yeovil Town station tender-first and then go onto the shed and turn ready for its return working to Salisbury.

ABOVE AND RIGHT Two views taken on Saturday 2 September 1961 of 'Merchant Navy' 4-6-2 No 35020 *Bibby Line* approaching with a down train and restarting from the down platform. The first set of coaches is still in the earlier BR red and cream replaced as soon as possible by the Southern Region with green. Alongside is 'S15' 4-6-0 No 30845, which has reversed its coaches into the down sidings. As will be seen in other photographs of the east end of Yeovil Junction station, the shunting signal for the movement from the lines behind the down platform was normally left off. The down main banner signal will be noticed on the end of the up signal gantry - this was installed when the down starting signals seen in the second picture were renewed in the early 1950s and were no longer tall enough to be sighted over the station footbridge by down express trains. The fireman having given the driver the right away is taking a breather as the driver opens the regulator and with steam sanders on No 35020 seems to have set the train in motion without slipping.

Two views, again on 2 September 1961, of the push-pull shuttle between Yeovil Junction and Yeovil Town stations comprising M7 0-4-4T No 30129 and one of the sets formed from surplus rolling stock after the Kent electrification.

FACING PAGE TOP From an elevated viewpoint No 30129 is seen approaching Yeovil Junction station from Yeovil Town with another train visible on the embankment in the distance. The footpath in the foreground is the long-lifted track of the connection from the Great Western Yeovil to Weymouth line to its Clifton Maybank goods station adjacent to the south side of Yeovil Junction station.

FACING PAGE BOTTOM Framed by the Newton Road bridge at the east end of Yeovil Town station, No 30129 propels its train towards Yeovil Junction station. The single line connection between Yeovil Town and Yeovil Pen Mill station can be seen on the left and the mixture of Southern and Great Western signalling is the result of the post-nationalisation indecision as to whether these lines were part of the Southern or Western Regions!

ABOVE The classic view looking north from Summer House Hill of Yeovil Town station and the shed was also taken on 2 September 1961. In front of the signalbox can be seen the single line with two platform faces used by the Yeovil Pen Mill to Taunton services. The island platform was used by services to Yeovil Junction and was only four coaches long. The goods yard to the left is busy as usual with two railway lorries and the normal collection of parcels vans, another raft of which is about to be shunted by the 'S15' 4-6-0 on the right. There are an interesting variety of eight-wheeled tenders on the 'S15' 4-6-0s and an unrebuilt Bulleid Pacific is visible on the right.

A unusual view of Yeovil Town shed looking west from the Newton Road on 27 April 1963. The three engines nearest to us are GWR 0-6-0PT No 8745, GWR 2-6-2T No 5548 and SR 'U' 2-6-0 No 31632. The influx of Great Western locomotives was the result of the closure of their small shed at Yeovil Pen Mill. The GWR locomotives were used on Yeovil to Taunton services and local and banking duties on the Castle Cary to Weymouth line. The men preparing the Bulleid Pacific in the background have allowed the safety valves to lift and, in the foreground, one member of the shed staff has found a quiet corner for a smoke out of sight of the foreman.

'West Country' 4-6-2 No 34026 *Yes Tor* has the road, but not the right away from its stop at Chard Junction with a down Yeovil Junction to Exeter passenger train on Saturday 8 September 1962. The large building to the right is a creamery and the engineer's train in front of it has an interesting pre-grouping coach possibly of South Eastern Railway origin. The gentleman with the raincoat on the right and the gathering on the up platform are mourners for the last day of passenger service on the Taunton to Ilminster and Chard line awaiting the 5.4pm departure from the separate platform out of sight to the left of this picture.

FACING PAGE Mark paid a visit to the Lyme Regis branch on Saturday 5 March 1960 with Maurice Deane by car. Here 'Merchant Navy' 4-6-2 No 35018 *British India Line* draws into Axminster station with a down express train while the branch locomotive, Adams radial 4-4-2T No 30583, has uncoupled from its coach in the bay platform ready to run round and return to Lyme Regis. The second picture shows how well kept the engine was, considering it was built in 1885 and had been sold to, and re-purchased from the Kent & East Sussex Railway.

ABOVE Ivatt 2-6-2T No 41292 tackles the horseshoe curve between Axminster and Combpyne with the five corridor coaches from Waterloo to Lyme Regis on Saturday 19 August 1961. This service would previously have been worked by two Adams radial tanks, one that had worked the branch on the previous week and would then return to Exmouth Junction while the second took over for the next week. Some tight 10 chain curves that were the reason for the retention of the radial tanks, were eased to allow the longer wheelbase 2-6-2 tanks to work the line.

ABOVE On the afternoon of Saturday 19 November 1960, Adams radial 4-4-2T No 30582 is seen heading towards Lyme Regis having just crossed the Cannington Viaduct. The structural problems with the concrete viaduct are very evident, with the strengthened arch and the subsidence at the Axminster end, however these date from the original construction of the line in 1903.

FACING PAGE Two views of Lyme Regis station: first Adams radial 4-4-2T No 30583 on 5 March 1960 seen from the buffer stops looking back towards Axminster with the porter engaged in conversation with the locomotive crew. A healthy goods traffic is evident with coal and van traffic on the right and a van in the loading dock on the left but, by February 1964, this service would cease and the sidings would be lifted. The pattern of the valancing on the station awning is noteworthy as are the three barrows awaiting passenger luggage. The second view in November 1960 shows one of the other two 4-4-2Ts, No 30582, departing past the small signalbox with more detail of the loading dock siding on the right.

ABOVE After initial dieselisation in 1964, shortage of units caused a resumption of steam operation using Great Western autocoaches, but without push-pull working. Here Ivatt 2-6-2T No 41216 arrives at Lyme Regis on 3 March 1965 with the service from Axminster. By this time the branch was worked as one 'engine in steam' and the only track at Lyme Regis was the locomotive run round. Mark recorded that on his journey to and from Lyme Regis to Axminster, in the up direction he was the only passenger and in the down direction, one child joined the train at the intermediate station Combpyne! Later, in March 1965, following closure of the Halwill to Torrington line, single-car diesel-units were used until closure of the branch in November 1965.

FACING PAGE TOP Back on the main line, rebuilt 'Merchant Navy' 4-6-2 No 35003 *Royal Mail* sweeps through Seaton Junction with the 11 coaches of the 10.48am Torrington to Waterloo on Saturday 17 August 1963. This was a high speed stretch for up trains, and hard work in prospect for down trains with six miles ahead at 1 in 70 to climb from the River Axe

valley at Seaton Junction to Honiton and the valley of the River Sid. Seaton Junction was rebuilt in the 1930s with separate platform and through roads and the famous 'sky' signals installed for sighting purposes.

FACING PAGE BOTTOM Four trains at Seaton Junction on Saturday 17 August 1963 for the price of one: reading from right to left we see 'S15' 4-6-0 No 30843 rolling into the up platform with an Exeter to Yeovil stopping train; then the rear coach and tail lamp of the down 'Atlantic Coast Express' headed by 'Merchant Navy' 4-6-2 No 35016 *Elders Fyffes*; the third train has 'Battle of Britain' 4-6-2 No 34083 *605 Squadron* which has just worked tender first from Seaton with 10.20am train to Waterloo. Having run through the branch platform to the left, when the road is clear it will run forward onto the down line and propel its coaches into the up platform and run round; finally GWR 0-6-0PT No 6412 with its two auto coaches has drawn forward into the headshunt and, when No 34083 has cleared, will return to shuttle to and from Seaton.

ABOVE The Station Master at Seaton Junction is on duty as the driver of 'S15' 4-6-0 No 30828 looks back for the right away to start the four coaches of the 1.35 pm Yeovil Junction to Exeter Central stopping passenger train on its way. Meanwhile on the up main 'Merchant Navy' 4-6-2 No 35030 *Elder Dempster Line* sweeps through with the feather-weight seven coaches of the 12.40 am Torrington to Waterloo. The date is again Saturday 17 August 1963.

FACING PAGE TOP Observed at Seaton Junction at 5.30pm on Saturday 8 August 1964 is the Okehampton to Surbiton car train with its normal formation of three coaches (including a restaurant car) and eight Covereed Carriage Trucks for cars The motive power is a very dirty 'Merchant Navy' 4-6-2 No 35029 *Ellerman Lines* which has steam to spare after the downhill run from Honiton.

FACING PAGE BOTTOM The branch platform was opened in February 1927 as part of the reconstruction of Seaton Junction station. Previously the branch trains had used a down bay platform involving a reversal when arriving or leaving. Here 'M7' 0-4-4T No 30048 has one of the 1960s push-pull sets on Saturday 5 March 1960 as it arrives from Seaton past milk tanks in the siding.

The same locomotive, No 30048, restarts its train from Colyton, one of the two intermediate stations towards Seaton on 19 August 1961. The driver can be clearly seen in the forward compartment and the advantage of the LSWR air system over the GWR mechanical system can be appreciated as a strengthening coach of LSWR origin has been added. A maximum of two coaches could be worked by the GWR mechanical system. A healthy goods traffic is evident from the sidings visible on the left of the picture.

On Saturday 5 March 1960, 'M7' 0-4-4T No 30048 leaves Seaton with a Seaton Junction service. The bleakness of the scenery is more like Dovey Junction, in west Wales, than the south coast and this appears to be one of the places where Southern Railway investment in facilities was never really rewarded. The through coaches to Waterloo ceased at the end of 1963, and even the last train in March 1966 was only patronised by a dozen passengers. However the trackbed of the branch, from Seaton to Colyton, was given a new use when the miniature electric trams were transferred from Eastbourne and the Seaton District Tramway was opened in August 1970.

Three pictures on Honiton Bank on Saturday 8 August 1964

ABOVE 'Battle of Britain' 4-6-2 No 34051 *Winston Churchill* is seen again, here tackling the 1 in 70 near mile post 151 with the 11 coaches of the 10.15am Waterloo to Ilfracombe and Torrington.

FACING PAGE TOP Later in the day, the weather deteriorated and BR Standard Class 5 4-6-0 No 73085 on the 11.45am Waterloo to Ilfracombe has clearly been through a heavy shower and, with its load of 12 coaches, the driver has started the steam sanding to maintain adhesion. This engine was allocated to Nine Elms at this time and so has presumably worked through from Waterloo.

FACING PAGE BOTTOM 'Battle of Britain' 4-6-2 No 34054 *Lord Beaverbrook* sweeps down past the signals of Honiton Incline signalbox with the 10 coaches of the 10.48am Torrington to Waterloo.

The fireman of 'West Country' 4-6-2 No 34015 *Exmouth* watches with interest as the engine is coupled up to the coaches of the 11.20am from Sidmouth in Sidmouth Junction station on 7 August 1965. No 34015 had worked light engine from Exmouth Junction shed and will now draw the coaches forward to await the Exmouth portion. On this day the Exmouth coaches were late arriving so that the departure was 16 minutes late but, with a trailing load of 350 tons, Mark recorded an excellent run to Salisbury regaining much of this lateness.

Ivatt 2-6-2T No 41224 is signalled into the down main platform as it approaches Sidmouth Junction from Tipton St John's with the three coaches of the 9.10am Littleham to Waterloo on Saturday 8 August 1964. It was followed by BR 2-6-2T No 82042 with the 9.30am Sidmouth portion and a few minutes later by the 9.30am Exmouth portion double-headed by BR 2-6-4T No 80043 and 2-6-2T No 82035 coupled bunker to bunker. The three portions having been assembled, 'Battle of Britain' 4-6-2 No 34079 *141 Squadron* was coupled on and here starts the train away for Waterloo from Sidmouth Junction. On the up main in the distance can be seen one of the tank engines and in the sidings to the left a 'Warship' diesel-hydraulic is lurking. During the day, Mark noted that three Exeter to Yeovil trains were operated by diesel-multiple units and one 'Warship' made a journey to Salisbury and back.

Rush Hour at Tipton St John's on Saturday 19 August 1961

ABOVE Ivatt 2-6-2T No 41299 and BR 2-6-2T No 84021 running bunker first bring the five coaches of the Sidmouth portion of the Cleethorpes train across the level crossing into Tipton St John's station. Unlike other trains from the branches which were combined at Sidmouth Junction, the Cleethorpes working was combined at Tipton St John's and then reversed at Sidmouth Junction travelling forward via Templecombe and the Somerset & Dorset Joint Railway until September 1962.

FACING PAGE TOP Locomotives Nos 41299 and 84021 then drew forward onto the single line to allow the five coaches from Exmouth, hauled by Ivatt 2-6-2T No 41270, into the station. The Sidmouth coaches were then reversed onto the Exmouth

portion to be worked forward by Nos 41299 and 84021. What road users of the level crossing at the Sidmouth end of the station thought of nearly an hour of movements is not recorded!

FACING PAGE BOTTOM Once the Cleethorpes had cleared the section, BR 2-6-2T No 82025 with a Sidmouth Junction to Sidmouth train could call at Tipton St John's and start to climb the 1 in 45 bank with driver waving to the photographer. In the background can be seen the aftermath of the Cleethorpe's train with an engine on the Exmouth line to the left and two engines in the headshunts at the other end of the station.

Note: Various references I have consulted spell the station as Tipton St John, Tipton St Johns and Tipton St John's in the 1909 LSWR Working Timetable which is the one I have used.

BR 2-6-2T No 82019 working on the Exmouth branch service from Exeter Central awaits its departure time at Exmouth on 31 March 1961 under the splendid array of LSWR signals. At this time the station reflected completely the 1924 rebuilding when the western island platform at which the train is standing was added to the existing island platform. The western platform was then used for the Exeter trains and the eastern platform for the Budleigh Salterton and Sidmouth Junction trains. The Budleigh Salterton line can be seen curving to the right beyond the signalbox with the connection to the goods yard in the foreground crossing the passenger lines.

BR 2-6-2T No 82010 runs into Topsham station with an Exmouth to Exeter Central train on Friday 31 March 1961. The siding off the headshunt on the right was the beginning of the Topsham Quay branch of 32 chains which led to the Quay on the River Exe. The siding was closed and lifted in 1957. It will be noted that there seemed to be no preferred direction of running of tank engines – a slight preference for running chimney towards Exmouth seems to be identifiable from a variety of photographs.

ABOVE There is a difference of about 100 feet between rail level at Exeter Central and Exeter St David's stations which meant a gradient of 1 in 37 for the connecting line. In the first photograph, taken at the south west end of Exeter Central on 15 April 1963, we are looking under the Queen Street road bridge and banking locomotive 'W class' 2-6-4T No 31916 can be seen having crossed from the up platform road in the foreground to the down road to return to Exeter St Davids. In the sidings behind, an unrebuilt Bulleid Pacific waits with a van and coach while to its left an 'M7' 0-4-4T is on duty as station pilot.

FACING PAGE The next two pictures are taken from the Bonhay Road on the same date as an unidentified 'West Country' 4-6-2 with a seven-coach portion of the up 'Atlantic Coast Express' is banked from Exeter St Davids station by 'W' class 2-6-2T No 31916. In the foreground on the left is Bob Griffiths, a fellow member of Bristol Railway Circle and Mark's companion on a number of railway photographic expeditions. Swinging round for the second picture the train engine has disappeared into the short tunnel under St David's Hill and the banker is about to cross the viaduct. The fencing shows an application of Exmouth Junction concrete products, there is a vintage display of adverts on the hoarding and it is a sobering thought that the young lady is probably now drawing her old age pension!

FACING PAGE TOP Looking south in the down Great Western and up Southern direction, 'West Country' 4-6-2 No 34011 *Tavistock* draws into Exeter St Davids station on Sunday 16 September 1962 with a train for the Plymouth direction. Unusually there is no entry in Mark's trip book for this visit which may mean that it was one of his regular visits to observe train operations at Exeter which continued regularly for over 50 years.

FACING PAGE BOTTOM SR Class N 2-6-0 No 31842 restarts its train in the Crediton direction from Exeter St Davids on Sunday 9 June 1963. This was one of the 50 engines built at Ashford in 1924 and 1925 from parts purchased by the Southern Railway from Woolwich Arsenal. The smokebox shows evidence of priming and the overall appearance is rather careworn. The signal gantry

in the background shows that rationalisation has begun with the removal of some arms and the running in board on the left EXETER (ST. DAVIDS) is different from the one in the previous picture (EXETER S^T DAVIDS).

ABOVE After the departure of the 'E1R' 0-6-2 tanks, and before the arrival of the 'W' 2-6-4 tanks, the 'Z' class 0-8-0 tanks were on banking duty at Exeter St Davids. Here 'Z' 0-8-0T No 30956 is easing up to bank a goods train up to Exeter Central on Monday October 1962 - in fact this train was heavy enough for the second 'Z' class tank on duty, No 30955, to act as pilot to 'N' class 2-6-0 No 31847. One therefore suspects that this might have been a Meldon granite train.

Two pictures of the shunting at Okehampton involved with the uniting of the Plymouth, Bude and Padstow portions of the 'Atlantic Coast Express' on Saturday 8 June 1963. 'West Country' 4-6-2 No 34002 *Salisbury* (which is shown on page XXZ (picture SWW110) brought the three coaches of the Padstow portion to Halwill Junction, where the five coaches that left Bude at 9.30am were attached – three for Waterloo and two for Okehampton. On arrival at Okehampton, the train engine, No 34002, was detached and pilot engine,

'N' class 2-6-0 No 31841, drew the train back into the up siding. The Plymouth portion of three coaches arrived behind 'N' class 2-6-0 No 31843 and the pilot reversed the Padstow and Bude portions onto the Plymouth portion and uncoupled the two Okehampton coaches. No 34002 now resumed its place at the head of the train comprising nine coaches as far as Exeter Central where one coach was removed and the train was worked forward at 12.20pm by 'Merchant Navy' 4-6-2 No 35026 *Lamport & Holt Line* to Waterloo.

ABOVE Rebuilt 'West Country' 4-6-2 No 34104 *Bere Alston*, in poor external condition, works a Plymouth to Exeter passenger service past Meldon Junction, to the west of Okehampton, on Tuesday 22 August 1961. This was the last Bulleid Pacific built at Eastleigh and also the last to be rebuilt in May 1961 whence it returned to Exmouth Junction shed being transferred to Eastleigh in November 1961. At first, rebuilt light Bulleid Pacifics were not allowed west of Okehampton or north of Crediton but this was later relaxed allowing them to reach Plymouth. 'Merchant Navy' Pacifics were never allowed west of Exeter. The line to Halwill Junction can be seen on the embankment to the right of the picture level with the buffer beam of the locomotive.

FACING PAGE TOP LSWR 'T9' 4-4-0 No 30338 arrives at Bere Alston with a Plymouth to Exeter train in May 1960. The line to Gunnislake and Callington drops away to the right and an unidentified 'O2' 0-4-4T shunts the sidings on the right indicating a healthy level of goods traffic. The notices in the foreground still have the L&SWR painted in white – a comparable picture six years later shows the passenger notices with red background and only the SR painted white and the bridge structure number has changed from black number and edging with white background to white numerals and edging and green background.

FACING PAGE BOTTOM A little earlier on the same day as the previous picture, the LSWR 'O2' 0-4-4T struggles up from Calstock viaduct to Bere Alston with a featherweight load of two 13-ton steel mineral wagons and a brakevan. In the distance above the engine can be seen Kit Hill with its ornate mine chimney

Mark followed Ivatt 2-6-2T No 41316 on a Sunday morning working on 27 August 1961 from Callington to Gunnislake. The line was rebuilt to standard gauge under a light railway order over this section on the track of the 3ft 6in gauge East Cornwall Mineral Railway in 1908 with Col H. F. Stephens as engineer. Beyond Gunnislake a new railway was built across Calstock viaduct to Bere Alston station.

Two views of the terminus at Callington station which is actually about one mile north of Callington proper at a village called Kelly Bray. The construction material of choice on this line was corrugated iron. Looking towards the buffers the overall roof can be seen which originally extended over the siding on which the two spare coaches are standing to the left. The view looking forward shows the small signalbox and engine shed and the edge of Kit Hill in the background.

RIGHT Luckett station was originally named Stoke Climsland in 1908 but was changed to Luckett in November 1909 following local complaints from the Stoke Climsland community (and especially the Vicar!) that it was misleading. The corrugated iron construction of the station building and wooden supports of the awning were of identical design to the building design at Calstock. Of perhaps more interest is the building on the right which was originally an East Cornwall Mineral Railway depot called Monk's Corner.

LEFT Gunnislake station is actually at Drakewalls a half mile south and 300 feet higher than Gunnislake proper. The station buildings date from the reconstruction of the line in 1908. This station was closed in 1994 and a replacement opened on the opposite, eastern, side of the A390 Tavistock to Callington Road allowing a low bridge to be removed. The difficulties of crossing the River Tamar by road make this still a popular rail service for commuters into Plymouth.

79

ABOVE 'N' class 2-6-0 No 31844 approaches Halwill Junction station from Okehampton on Saturday 8 June 1963 with a passenger train. The terrain following nature of the line can be seen in the background. Of interest is the first vehicle a long wheelbase four-wheeled van with guard look-out duckets, possibly LNER in origin maybe even pre-grouping.

FACING PAGE TOP As noted in an earlier caption, 'West Country' 4-6-2 No 34002 *Salisbury* worked the three coaches of the Padstow portion of the 'Atlantic Coast Express' on Saturday 8 August 1963 and here it arrives at Halwill Junction viewed from the North Devon & Cornwall Junction platform. The five coaches from Bude are ready to be attached to the rear of the Padstow coaches. The fireman of No 34002 is standing behind the driver ready to hand over the single-line tablet to the signalman.

FACING PAGE BOTTOM Trains meet at Tresmeer on Monday 3 June 1963 on the North Cornwall line between Halwill Junction and Wadebridge. 'Battle of Britain' 4-6-2 No 34083 *605 Squadron* on an up Wadebridge to Okehampton passenger train, is crossing 'West Country' 4-6-2 No 34030 *Watersmeet* on the Padstow coaches of the 'Atlantic Coast Express' which started their journey at Waterloo at 11am and will not reach Wadebridge, a further 23 miles away, until 5.07pm. Mark has left the coach door open, knowing he can take his photograph as No 34030 will not start until the tablet has been surrendered for the single line section which No 34083 has just cleared.

ABOVE Class 'T9' 4-4-0 No 30717 awaits the signal for the line at Padstow at Wadebridge with a train from Bodmin North on Monday 11 July 1960. The engine was built by Dubs & Co at Glasgow in 1899 to the designs of Dugald Drummond and was fitted with a superheated boiler in 1927. It survived another year after this picture. In the background on the left can be seen Wadebridge engine shed which must qualify as one of the cleanest in the country!

FACING PAGE TOP 'N' class 2-6-0 No 31855 will not be able to leave the east end of Wadebridge station with its Padstow to Okehampton train until Ivatt 2-6-2T No 41275 with its two-coach train for Bodmin North clears the crossover. The North Cornwall line to Halwill Junction and the Bodmin line were both

single track but ran parallel for about ¾-mile east of Wadebridge until the Halwill Junction line swung north across the River Camel to follow the valley of the River Allen. The date is Monday 3 June 1963.

FACING PAGE BOTTOM At Boscarne Junction the line from the Great Western Railway at Bodmin General joined the original Wadebridge to Bodmin North line. Mark is standing by the Bodmin General line in the foreground, with Boscarne Junction signalbox in the distance, the line to Wadebridge straight ahead and that to Bodmin North and Wenford Bridge behind the small cabin of Boscarne Ground Frame. The sidings allowed wagons to and from Bodmin North for the Great Western line at Bodmin Road (now Bodmin Parkway) to avoid congesting the yard at Wadebidge.

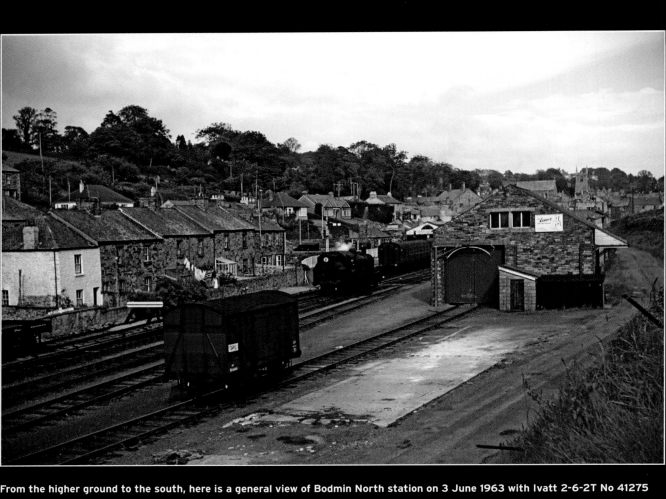

From the higher ground to the south, here is a general view of Bodmin North station on 3 June 1963 with Ivatt 2-6-2T No 41275 running round its two-coach train ready to return to Wadebridge. The substantial goods shed is no longer in railway use having been taken over by an animal feed merchant who still apparently uses the railway for supplies. It would appear that most of the buildings date from the 1895 reconstruction of the original Bodmin & Wadebridge terminus using local stone completely in character with the houses in the background.

As No 34072 runs round and makes its way to the shed and turntable in the far left, the demanding nature of the start from
Ilfracombe station can be seen. The incline at 1 in 36 starts at the platform end and continues for three miles to Mortehoe station.
No 34072 will in due course tackle it with the three coaches of the 4.50pm departure to Barnstaple Junction.

Index of locations

Index of locomotive classes